All American Dessert Cookbook

Recipes Reflecting the American Spirt

Volume 2

Copyright Material

© 2023 Steven Masters

All Rights Reserved

No part of this book may be used or transmitted in any form or by any means without the proper written consent of the publisher and copyright owner, except for brief quotations used in a review. This book should not be considered a substitute for medical, legal, or other professional advice.

Sign-up Now
and Be Notified of New Books

Website: readbooks.today

Table of Contents

COOKIES — 1

BISCOCHITOS	2
BY CRACKY BARS	3
COWBOY COOKIES	4
HERMIT COOKIES	6
LEMON BAR	7
NANAIMO BARS	8
PEANUT BUTTER BROWNIES	9
SNICKERDOODLES	10
WHOOPIE PIES	11

CAKES — 13

CHIFFON CAKE	14
CHEESECAKE	15
BLACKBERRY CAKE	17
COCONUT CAKE	19
DAIRY QUEEN ICE CREAM CAKE	21
DEVILS' FOOD CAKE	23
GERMAN CHOCOLATE CAKE	25
JUNIOR'S CHEESECAKE	27
LANE CAKE	29
HERSHEY'S CHOCOLATE CHEESECAKE	32
NEW YORK CHEESECAKE	33
SMITH ISLAND CAKE	35
TEXAS SHEET CAKE	37
TUNNEL OF FUDGE CAKE	39
STRAWBERRY SHORTCAKE	41

PIES — 42

APPLE PIE	43
BLACK BOTTOM PIE	45
BLUEBERRY PIE	46
BUMBLEBERRY PIE	47
CHERRY PIE	48
CHIFFON PIE	49

Coconut Custard Pie	50
Derby Pie	51
Grape Pie	52
Jelly Cream Pie	53
Huckleberry Pie	55
Lemon Chiffon Pie	56
Mississippi Mud Pie	57
Pecan Pie	59
Rhubarb Pie	60
Shoofly Pie	61
Strawberry Rhubarb Pie	62
Sweet Potato Pie	63

PUDDING — 64

Butter Scotch Pudding	65
Hasty Pudding	66
Persimmon Pudding	67
Tapioca Pudding	68
Waldorf Pudding	69

CANDY — 70

Buckeyes	71
Honeycomb Toffee	72
Peanut Butter Fudge	73
Snickers Salad	74

Cookies

Biscochitos

Prep Time: 30 minutes
Cooking Time: 20 minutes
Servings: 30

Ingredients

- 6 cups flour
- 1 ½ cups sugar
- 2 teaspoons anise seed
- 1-pound lard
- 2 large eggs
- ¼ cup sugar
- 1 tablespoon cinnamon
- 3 teaspoons baking powder
- ½ cup sweet table wine
- 1 teaspoon salt

Directions

1. Sift the flour with baking powder & salt in a large-sized mixing bowl until mixed well. Cream the lard with anise seed and sugar on medium speed.
2. Once done; beat the eggs in a separate bowl until light & fluffy. Add the beaten eggs into the creamed mixture. Mix well; add wine to form stiff-like dough. Feel free to add more of wine, if needed.
3. Refrigerate the prepared dough for overnight, covered.
4. The following day; preheat your oven to 350F.
5. Remove the dough carefully from your refrigerator & let stand for a couple of minutes until soft enough to roll.
6. Evenly divide the dough into quarters & roll each to approximately ⅛" thickness. Cut with the cookie cutter & arrange on the cookie sheet. Bake in the preheated oven until bottom of the cookies turn golden brown, for 12 to 15 minutes.
7. In the meantime, combine the cinnamon with sugar in a separate bowl. Drop the baked cookies carefully into the cinnamon-sugar mix & set aside to cool.

By Cracky Bars

Prep Time: 20 minutes
Cooking Time: 30 minutes
Servings: 24

Ingredients

- 2 large eggs
- ¾ cup shortening
- 1 cup semi-sweet chocolate chips
- 1 ¾ cups flour
- ¼ teaspoon baking soda
- 1 cup sugar
- 1/3 cup milk
- 1 teaspoon vanilla extract
- ¾ cup walnuts, chopped
- 1-ounce unsweetened chocolate, melted
- 9 whole graham crackers
- 1 teaspoon salt

Directions

1. Preheat your oven to 375F.
2. Cream the shortening with sugar.
3. Add the eggs & beat on low speed until mixed well.
4. Next, combine the flour with soda and salt. Add to the creamed mix alternately with the milk; don't forget to mix well after each addition.
5. Add in the vanilla; give it a good stir.
6. Place ⅓ of the prepared batter in a separate bowl & stir in the walnuts and melted chocolate into this.
7. Spread the chocolate mixture into a greased, large pan.
8. Arrange graham crackers on top of the batter.
9. Add chocolate morsels to the leftover batter & drop over the crackers by the spoonful, carefully spread and ensure that it's nicely covered.
10. Bake in the preheated oven for 25 minutes.
11. Let cool and then, cut into desired bars. Enjoy.

Cowboy Cookies

Prep Time: 20 minutes
Cooking Time: 20 minutes
Servings: 31

Ingredients

- 1 ¾ cups unbleached all-purpose flour; scoop & leveled
- 1 teaspoon ground cinnamon
- 2 cups rolled oats (not quick oats)
- 1 cup light brown sugar, packed
- ½ cup granulated sugar
- 1 cup unsalted butter, at room temperature
- 2 large eggs
- 1 ¼ cups toasted pecans, chopped
- 2 cups semi-sweet chocolate chips, divided
- 1 ½ cups moist sweetened coconut, shredded
- 2 teaspoons vanilla extract
- 1 teaspoon baking soda
- ¾ teaspoon salt

Directions

1. Whisk the flour with cinnamon, baking soda and salt in a large-sized mixing bowl until mixed well. Set aside.
2. Next, cream the butter with granulated sugar and brown sugar in the bowl of an electric stand mixer attached to a paddle until blended well.
3. Slowly mix in the eggs; beat well after each addition and then, mix the vanilla. Scrapping the sides & bottom of your bowl down, as needed.
4. Add the prepared flour mixture; continue to combine the ingredients until mixed well.
5. Add the oats followed by 1 ½ cups of chocolate chips, pecans, and coconut; continue to mix the ingredients.
6. Cover the bowl & let the dough to chill for an hour, until less sticky & easy to work with. During the last 15 minutes of chilling time; preheat your oven to 350F.
7. Scoop out approximately 3 tablespoons of dough at a time and roll into balls: pressing the leftover chocolate chips into 6" dough balls.

8. Transfer 12 formed balls to the parchment paper lined with the baking sheet, evenly spaced. Keep the leftover dough in the fridge until needed.
9. Slightly flatten the balls of dough and then, bake for 14 to 16 minutes, until cookies appear set on edges & lightly golden brown on the bottom.
10. Let cool on the baking sheet for a couple of minutes and then, transfer them to a wire rack to completely cool. Repeat these cooking steps with the leftover cookie dough and store the baked cookies in an airtight container.

Hermit Cookies

Prep Time: 20 minutes
Cooking Time: 30 minutes
Servings: 48

Ingredients

- 2 eggs, large
- 1 cup packed brown sugar
- ½ teaspoon vanilla extract
- 1 ¾ cups all-purpose flour
- ½ teaspoon salt
- 1 cup coarsely pecans or walnuts, chopped
- ½ tsp cinnamon
- 1 cup dates, chopped
- ⅛ teaspoon allspice
- 1 cup raisins
- ½ cup softened butter, at room temperature
- 1 teaspoon baking soda

Directions

1. Preheat your oven to 350F.
2. Cream the butter with brown sugar in a standing mixer on medium speed. Add the eggs & continue to beat for 2 minutes, until mixture is thick and pale. Beat in the vanilla.
3. Decrease the speed of your mixer to low & beat in the nutmeg, flour, baking soda, allspice, cinnamon, and salt until mixed well. Incorporate the raisins, nuts, and dates.
4. Using tablespoonfuls; drop the cookies onto a baking sheet lined with parchment or well-greased, approximately 2 apart. Bake until the edges are set but centers are still moist, for 10 to 12 minutes. Let cool on the baking sheet for 2 minutes and then, transfer them to wire racks to completely cool. Enjoy.

Lemon Bar

Prep Time: 20 minutes
Cooking Time: 40 minutes
Servings: 24

Ingredients

For Crust:
- 1 cup softened butter, at room temperature
- 2 cups all-purpose flour
- ½ cup white sugar

For Filling:
- 4 large eggs
- ¼ cup all-purpose flour
- Juice of 2 lemons, fresh
- 1 ½ cups white sugar

Directions

1. Preheat your oven to 350F.
2. For Crust: Blend 2 cups of flour with ½ cup of sugar, and the softened butter in a medium-sized mixing bowl until mixed well; press into the bottom of an ungreased, large pan.
3. Bake for 15 minutes, until firm & golden. In the meantime, prepare the filling. Whisk the leftover sugar with ¼ cup of flour in a medium-sized mixing bowl. Whisk in the eggs and then, the lemon juice until completely smooth; pour the filling on top of the baked crust.
4. Bake for 20 more minutes. Set aside to completely cool and then, cut into desired squares.

Nanaimo Bars

Prep Time: 30 minutes
Cooking Time: 30 minutes
Servings: 16

Ingredients

- 4 squares semisweet baking chocolate (1 ounce)
- 1 cup butter, softened, divided
- 2 cups confectioners' sugar
- ¼ cup white sugar
- 2 tablespoons custard powder
- 1 beaten egg, large
- 3 tablespoons heavy cream
- 1 ¾ cups graham cracker crumbs
- 2 teaspoons butter
- 1 cup flaked coconut
- 5 tablespoons cocoa powder, unsweetened
- ½ cup almonds, finely chopped, optional

Directions

1. Combine ½ cup of softened butter with the cocoa powder & sugar in the top of a double boiler until smooth and melted, stirring occasionally. Beat in the egg & stir for 2 to 3 minutes, until thick.
2. Remove from the heat & mix in the almonds, graham cracker crumbs, and coconut. Press into the bottom of an ungreased, large pan.
3. For Middle Layer: Beat the leftover softened butter with custard powder, and heavy cream until light & fluffy.
4. Mix in the confectioners' sugar until completely smooth. Spread over the bottom layer. Let chill until set.
5. Meanwhile, melt the semisweet chocolate with 2 teaspoons of butter over low heat or in the microwave.
6. Spread the melted chocolate mixture on top of the chilled bars. Let the chocolate set then cut into desired squares.

Peanut Butter Brownies

Prep Time: 20 minutes
Cooking Time: 30 minutes
Servings: 16

Ingredients

- ⅔ cup white sugar
- ½ cup peanut butter
- 2 eggs, large
- ½ teaspoon vanilla extract
- 1 cup all-purpose flour
- ⅓ cup softened margarine
- 1 teaspoon baking powder
- ½ cup brown sugar, packed
- ¼ teaspoon salt

Directions

1. Grease a large baking pan and then, preheat your oven to 350F.
2. Next, cream the margarine with peanut butter in a medium-sized mixing bowl until mixed well. Slowly blend in the white sugar, eggs, brown sugar, and vanilla; continue to mix until completely fluffy.
3. Combine the flour with baking powder & salt in a separate bowl. Once done; immediately stir into the prepared peanut butter mix until blended well.
4. Bake for 30 to 35 minutes, until the top springs back. Let cool and then, cut evenly into 16 squares.

Snickerdoodles

Prep Time: 40 minutes
Cooking Time: 20 minutes
Servings: 48

Ingredients

For Cookies:
- 1 ½ cups white sugar
- 2 large eggs
- ½ cup shortening
- 2 teaspoons vanilla extract
- 1 teaspoon baking soda
- 2 ¾ cups all-purpose flour
- ½ cup softened butter
- 2 teaspoons cream of tartar
- ¼ teaspoon salt

For Sugar- Cinnamon Coating:
- 2 teaspoons ground cinnamon
- 2 tablespoons white sugar

Directions

1. Preheat your oven to 400F.
2. For Cookies: Beat the butter with sugar, eggs, shortening, and vanilla in a large-sized mixing bowl until completely creamy & smooth.
3. Next, whisk the flour with baking soda, cream of tartar, and salt in a separate bowl. Slowly mix the dry ingredients mix into the wet ingredients until just combined. Shape the dough into walnut-sized balls.
4. For Sugar-Cinnamon Mix: Combine the cinnamon with sugar in a zip-top plastic bag or small bowl.
5. Place dough balls into the sugar-cinnamon & shake or roll until nicely coated. Place approximately 2" apart on baking sheets, ungreased.
6. Bake for 8 to 10 minutes, until set, switching the racks halfway.
7. Remove & immediately transfer to wire racks to completely cool.

Whoopie Pies

Prep Time: 20 minutes
Cooking Time: 20 minutes
Servings: 06

Ingredients

For Cookies:
- 1 cup white sugar
- 2 eggs, separated, divided
- 1 teaspoon baking soda
- 2 cups all-purpose flour
- 1 teaspoon baking powder
- 5 tablespoons unsweetened cocoa powder
- 1 cup milk
- ½ cup shortening
- 1 teaspoon vanilla extract
- ½ teaspoon salt

For Filling:
- 1 teaspoon vanilla extract
- ¾ cup shortening
- 2 cups confectioners' sugar
- A pinch of salt

Directions

1. Grease cookie sheets and then, preheat your oven to 350F.
2. For Cookies: Beat the sugar with egg yolks and shortening using an electric mixer in a large bowl until light & fluffy.
3. Sift the flour with cocoa, baking soda, baking powder, and salt in a separate bowl; work in batches & add to the shortening mixture, alternating with the milk; briefly beating after each addition until completely smooth. Stir in the vanilla. By the spoonful, drop dough onto the prepared baking sheets approximately 2" apart.
4. Bake for 10 to 15 minutes and then, transfer to a wire rack to completely cool.
5. For Filling: Beat the confectioners' sugar with reserved egg whites, shortening, and salt using an electric mixer in a large bowl until light & fluffy then, stir in the vanilla.
6. Choose 2 cookies of the same size; spread a thick layer of filling on the flat side of one cookie; top with the other cookie. Repeat with the leftover frosting and cookies. Enjoy.

Cakes

Chiffon Cake

Prep Time: 40 minutes
Cooking Time: 1 hour & 30 minutes
Servings: 14

Ingredients

- 1 tablespoon baking powder
- 2 cups cake flour, sifted
- 1 ½ cups white sugar
- 7 large eggs, separated, divided
- ½ teaspoon cream of tartar
- 2 teaspoons vanilla extract
- ¾ cup cold water
- 1 teaspoon lemon extract
- ½ cup vegetable oil
- 1 teaspoon salt

Directions

1. Wash a large, angel food tube pan in hot soapy water until grease-free; dry well and then, preheat your oven to 325F.
2. Next, measure the flour with baking powder, sugar, and salt into a sifter; sift into a large bowl. Make a well in middle; add the egg yolks followed by vanilla extract, oil, lemon extract, and water to the well. Don't beat.
3. Beat the egg whites with cream of tartar until very stiff in a separate, large-sized mixing bowl.
4. Beat the egg yolk batter using the same beaters until smooth & light; slowly pour on top of the egg whites. Gently fold the mixtures together using a rubber spatula; don't stir. Pour the batter into the tube pan.
5. Bake for 55 minutes. Once done; increase the oven's temperature to 350 F & bake for 12 to 15 minutes more, until a toothpick comes out clean.
6. Invert the pan carefully onto a wire rack. Let completely cool before unmolding & frosting as desired.

Cheesecake

Prep Time: 30 minutes
Cooking Time: 55 minutes
Servings: 08

Ingredients

- 2 tablespoons all-purpose flour
- 32 ounces full-fat cream cheese
- 5 large eggs
- 9 ½ ounces sugar, plus 1 tablespoon, divided
- 2 teaspoons vanilla extract
- 8 ounces heavy cream
- 2 yolks from 2 large eggs
- Zest of 1 lemon, finely grated
- 1 teaspoon kosher salt

Directions

1. Preheat your oven to 450F with the rack in middle. Cut two 12 by 16" pieces of parchment paper and arrange the parchment pieces in an overlapping pattern to line a greased 9x3" springform cake pan, leaving at least 2" of parchment overhanging the rim of the pan on all sides; set aside
2. Next, combine the cream cheese with sugar in the bowl of a stand mixer attached to the paddle. Mix for 3 to 5 minutes, until sugar is dissolved, no lumps of cheese remain, and mixture is completely smooth, on medium speed; scraping the sides of your bowl down, as required
3. With the mixer still running, slowly add the eggs, beating well after each addition. Add egg yolks & continue to beat for 15 seconds, until incorporated well; stopping the mixer & scrapping the sides of your bowl down using a rubber spatula. Ensure that the mix is completely smooth & homogenous
4. Add the flour, cream, vanilla, lemon zest, and salt. Continue to mix for 30 seconds, until smooth and fully combined, on medium speed. Pour the prepared batter into the pan & refrigerate for an hour
5. Once ready to bake, remove the cake pan from your refrigerator, place it on a rimmed baking sheet & evenly sprinkle with the leftover sugar on top of the batter. Bake for 25 to 30 minutes, cheesecake until the surface turns light brown and is starting to set around the edges. Rotate the baking sheet to ensure even browning, if needed
6. Increase your oven temperature to 500 F & continue to bake for 25 more minutes, until surface is burnished milk chocolate-brown & outer edge of your cheesecake feels slightly firm
7. Let the cheesecake to cool in the pan for 4 hours at room temperature before unmolding. Unlatch the springform pan & remove pan sides. Holding by parchment overhang, carefully transfer the cake to a large serving plate or cutting board. Gently peel the parchment from the sides of your cheesecake & cut into wedges using a sharp knife. Serve and enjoy.

Blackberry Cake

Prep Time: 20 minutes
Cooking Time: 30 minutes
Servings: 08

Ingredients

- 7 ounces fresh blackberries, firm & tart
- 1 ¼ teaspoons baking powder
- 5 ¼ ounces sugar
- ¼ teaspoon baking soda
- 2 ounces egg whites
- ⅛ teaspoon ground cinnamon
- 5 ½ ounces bleached cake flour, sifted
- ¼ teaspoon kosher salt
- 4 ounces unsalted butter, softened

To Serve:
- More of blackberries, to garnish
- 1 batch of cream cheese frosting

Directions

1. Purée the blackberries using a food processor, blender, or immersion blender until completely smooth. Measure 6 ounces of the fresh blackberry purée out and bring to approximately 70 F before you use it.
2. Next, preheat your oven to 350 F with the rack in lower-middle position. Lightly grease an 8x2" anodized aluminum cake pan & line it with the parchment.
3. For Cake: Combine the butter with baking soda, baking powder, sugar, cinnamon, and salt in the bowl of a stand mixer attached to the paddle. Mix until incorporated roughly, on low speed. Once done; increase the speed to medium & beat for 5 minutes, until light and fluffy. Pause & scrape the sides of your bowl and the beater using a flexible spatula approximately halfway during the process. With the mixer still running, slowly add the egg whites, letting each addition to incorporate completely before you proceed with the next
4. Decrease the speed to low & sprinkle in approximately ⅓ of the cake flour, followed by ⅓ of the prepared blackberry purée. Repeat with leftover flour & fruit
5. Scrape the beater and bowl down using a flexible spatula & continue to mix until incorporated well, for 3 seconds, on medium speed. Feel free to fold the batter using a flexible spatula; if it looks tie-dyed or streaky until streaks disappear
6. Scrape into the prepared pan, evenly spreading; bake for half an hour, until firm & puffed. Let cool directly in the pan for an hour and then, run a butter knife around the edges to loosen. Carefully invert onto a wire rack, peel the parchment off & place on a large serving plate for an hour, until completely cool. Top with a batch of cream cheese frosting & a handful of fresh blackberries. Cut into desired slices and enjoy.

Coconut Cake

Prep Time: 40 minutes
Cooking Time: 50 minutes
Servings: 12

Ingredients

- 2 cups sugar
- 1 ½ teaspoons pure vanilla extract
- 5 eggs, extra-large, at room temperature
- 1 ½ teaspoons pure almond extract
- 3 cups all-purpose flour, plus more for dusting the pans
- ¾ pound unsalted butter (3 sticks), at room temperature, plus additional for greasing
- 1 teaspoon baking powder
- ½ teaspoon baking soda
- 4 ounces sweetened shredded coconut
- 1 cup milk
- ½ teaspoon kosher salt

For Frosting:
- ½ pound unsalted butter (2 sticks), at room temperature
- 1-pound cream cheese, at room temperature
- ¾ teaspoon pure vanilla extract
- 6 ounces sweetened coconut, shredded
- 1-pound confectioners' sugar, sifted
- ¼ teaspoon pure almond extract

Directions

1. Grease 2 large round cake pans and then, line them each with the parchment paper. Grease and dust them lightly with the flour and then, preheat your oven to 350F.
2. Next, cream the butter with sugar in the bowl of an electric mixer attached to a paddle until fluffy and light yellow, for 3 to 5 minutes, on medium-high speed. Crack eggs into a small bowl. With the mixer still running on the medium speed, slowly add the eggs, scraping down the sides of your bowl once. Add the almond extracts and vanilla; continue to mix.
3. Sift the flour with baking soda, baking powder and salt in a separate bowl. With the mixer still running on low speed, alternately add the dry ingredients & the milk to the batter in three parts, starting and ending with the dry ingredients. Continue to mix until just combined. Fold in the 4 ounces of the coconut using a large rubber spatula.
4. Evenly pour the prepared batter into the 2 pans & smooth the top using a knife. Bake until a cake tester comes out clean, for 45 to 55 minutes. Let cool for 30 minutes on a baking rack and then, turn out the cakes onto a baking rack to end the cooling process.
5. For Frosting: Combine the cream cheese with butter, almond extract, and vanilla in the bowl of an electric mixer attached to a paddle, on low speed. Add the confectioners' sugar & continue to mix until just smooth.
6. To Assemble: Place 1-layer, top side down on a flat serving plate & spread with the frosting. Place the second layer (top side up) on top & frost the sides and top. Sprinkle the top with coconut & lightly press more of coconut onto the sides. Serve at room temperature. Enjoy.

Dairy Queen Ice Cream Cake

Prep Time: 30 minutes
Cooking Time: 5 hours & 10 minutes
Servings: 12

Ingredients

For Chocolate Cookie Crunchies
- ¾ cup Oreo crumbs
- 1 ½ tablespoons melted butter

For Chocolate Fudge
- 1 cup semi-sweet chocolate chips
- ½ teaspoon vanilla extract
- 3 tablespoons light corn syrup
- ½ cup heavy whipping cream

For Ice Cream Layers
- 1.5-quart container each of chocolate ice cream, and vanilla ice cream

For Whipped Cream
- 1 cup powdered sugar
- 2 cups heavy whipping cream, cold
- 1 ½ teaspoons vanilla extract
- Sprinkles

Directions

1. Line a large-sized cookie sheet with a silicone baking mat or the parchment paper; set aside and then, preheat your oven to 350F.
2. Next, combine the melted butter with Oreo crumbs; stir until mixed well. Evenly spread the crumbs over the cookie sheet.
3. Bake in the preheated oven for 8 to 10 minutes; let cool. Break any big clumps into smaller ones using your fingers; set aside.
4. Line a large cake pan with clear wrap. Ensure that the bottom is covered & the wrap goes above the sides of your cake pan.
5. Set the chocolate ice cream out to soften approximately 20 minutes prior to use it. Add the softened chocolate ice cream to the prepared cake pan & spread into an even layer. Freeze for half an hour.
6. For Fudge Layer: Add the corn syrup, vanilla extract, and chocolate chips to a medium sized mixing bowl.
7. Heat the heavy whipping cream until it just begins to boil and then, carefully pour it on top of the chocolate chips. Let sit for 2 to 3 minutes and then, whisk until completely smooth.
8. Remove the cake pan that has the chocolate ice cream from your freezer and then, pour the prepared chocolate fudge on top of the ice cream; evenly spreading. Freeze for 10 minutes.
9. Add the cookie crumbles over the fudge layer and then, freeze until mostly firm, for 2 hours.
10. Set the vanilla ice cream out to soften approximately 20 minutes prior to use it. Add the vanilla ice cream over the cake and then, freeze for 2 to 3 hours, until firm.
11. Carefully lift the frozen cake out of your pan using the clear wrap and then, place it on a serving plate or a cardboard cake circle. Place it inside the freezer again.
12. For Whipped Cream: Add the heavy whipping cream with vanilla extract and powdered sugar to a large-sized mixer bowl. Whip until stiff peaks form, on high speed.
13. Frost your cake with the whipped cream & garnish per your likings.
14. Freeze the cake until ready to serve

Devils' Food Cake

Prep Time: 2 hours & 20 minutes
Cooking Time: 1 hour & 50 minutes
Servings: 10

Ingredients

For Cake:
- 2 cups all-purpose unbleached flour
- ¾ cup non-alkalized cocoa powder (not Dutch-processed)
- 1 ½ teaspoons baking soda
- 12 tablespoons unsalted butter, at room temperature, plus additional for pans
- 2 cups plus 2 tablespoons sugar
- ¾ teaspoon baking powder
- 2 teaspoons pure vanilla extract
- ¼ cup milk
- 3 large eggs, at room temperature
- 1 ¼ cups water
- ¾ teaspoon salt

For Frosting:
- 1 ½ cups heavy cream
- 15 ounces finely chopped chocolate, semi-sweet

Directions

1. For Frosting: Fill a large heatproof bowl with the chocolate. Next, bring the cream to a boil in a small saucepan, over moderate heat. Pour the cream carefully on top of the chocolate; gently move the bowl and let the cream to settle. Set the mixture aside for 4 minutes, until softened. Whisk until completely smooth. Cover the surface of your frosting with the plastic wrap; set aside & let set up for 2 hours, at room temperature.
2. For Cake: Preheat your oven to 350 F with a rack in middle. Lightly coat two, large round cake pans with butter and line the bottoms with a circle of wax or parchment paper.
3. Whisk the flour with baking powder, baking soda, and salt in a medium-sized mixing bowl; set aside.
4.

5. Beat the butter in a standing mixer attached to the paddle for 2 minutes, until completely smooth, at medium speed. Increase the speed to medium-high & slowly add the sugar. Continue to beat for 4 minutes, until light & smooth. Turn off the mixer & scrape down the sides of your bowl using a rubber spatula. Add the vanilla and cocoa powder; continue to beat for a minute more, at medium speed; stopping & scrapping down the sides of your bowl, if required. With the mixer still running at medium-low speed, slowly add in the eggs; beat well for a minute after each addition. Don't forget to scrape down the sides of your bowl, as needed.
6. Next, over moderate heat in a saucepan; bring the milk and water just to a boil. Once done; remove the saucepan from heat.
7. With the mixer running at low speed, slowly add in the flour mixture. Pour the hot liquid carefully into the batter. Remove the bowl from mixer & finish combining the batter using a large rubber spatula until completely smooth. Evenly divide the batter between the prepared pans. Lightly drop each pan onto the counter to settle the batter.
8. Set the pans on the middle rack in the oven. Bake for 30 to 35 minutes, until the cakes begin to pull away from the sides of your pans.
9. Let the cakes to cool in the pans for 10 minutes on a rack. Turn out the cake layers of the pans & let cool on the rack.
10. To Assemble. Place 1 cake layer on a flat plate or cake stand, upside-down. Scoop approximately ⅓ of icing onto the center of the layer. Evenly spread the icing over the layer to the edges using a large, offset spatula. Place the other cake layer, rounded side up, on top. Spread half of the leftover icing evenly on top, spreading any excess icing down the sides. Spread the leftover icing around the sides of your cake. Make a swirling pattern in the icing using the tip of the offset spatula. Serve and enjoy.

German Chocolate Cake

Prep Time: 30 minutes
Cooking Time: 50 minutes
Servings: 16

Ingredients

For Chocolate Cake:
- 1 ¾ cups all-purpose flour
- 2 cups granulated sugar
- 1 ½ teaspoons baking powder
- ¾ cup unsweetened cocoa powder
- 1 cup buttermilk
- 2 organic eggs, large
- 1 ½ teaspoons baking soda
- ½ cup canola or vegetable oil
- 1 cup boiling water
- 2 teaspoons vanilla extract
- 1 teaspoon salt

For Coconut Frosting:
- 3 large egg yolks
- ½ cup butter
- 1 tablespoon vanilla extract
- ½ cup granulated sugar
- 1 cup pecans, chopped
- ¾ cup evaporated milk
- 1 cup sweetened coconut, shredded
- ½ cup light brown sugar

For Chocolate Frosting:
- ⅔ cup unsweetened cocoa powder
- 3 cups powdered sugar
- ½ cup butter
- 1 teaspoon vanilla extract
- ⅓ cup evaporated milk

Directions

1. Grease two large round baking pans; line the bottom with a round piece of parchment or wax paper and then, preheat your oven to 375F.

For Cake:
1. Stir the flour with baking soda, sugar, baking powder, cocoa, and salt in large-sized mixing bowl until mixed well. Combine the eggs with buttermilk, vanilla, and oil in a separate bowl & mix well. Add the mix of wet ingredients into the dry ingredients & continue to mix until mixed well. Stir in the boiling water. Fill the prepared pans evenly with the batter.
2. Bake until a toothpick comes out with few crumbs or completely clean, for 25 to 35 minutes. Let cool in the pan for 5 minutes and then carefully invert onto wire racks to completely cool.

For German Chocolate Frosting:
1. Add granulated sugar with brown sugar, egg yolks, butter, and evaporated milk in a medium-sized saucepan. Give it a good stir until combined well & bring the mix to a low boil, over moderate heat. Continue to stir until the mix starts to thicken, for a couple of minutes.
2. Remove from the heat & immediately stir in the nuts, coconut, and vanilla. Let completely cool before you begin with the layering process.

For Chocolate Buttercream Frosting:
1. Heat the butter until melted and then, stir in the cocoa powder. Alternately add milk and powdered sugar; beat until you get spreading-like consistency. Add a bit of more milk or powder, if required to adjust the frosting to your likings. Stir in the vanilla.

Cake Assembly:
1. Place one of the cake rounds on your serving plate or stand.
2. Smooth a thin layer of the prepared chocolate frosting on top of the cake layer and then, spoon approximately half of the prepared coconut frosting on top; evenly spreading. Leave approximately ½" between the edge & filling of your cake.
3. Stack the second cake round on top. Smooth chocolate frosting over the entire cake.
4. Spoon the leftover coconut frosting over the cake.

Junior's Cheesecake

Prep Time: 30 minutes
Cooking Time: 2 hours & 20 minutes
Servings: 12

Ingredients

For Sponge Cake Layer:
- 3 large eggs, separated
- ½ cup cake flour, sifted
- 3 tablespoons unsalted butter, melted
- 1 teaspoon baking powder
- 2 tablespoons sugar
- ⅓ cup sugar
- 3 drops of lemon extract
- 1 teaspoon pure vanilla extract
- ¼ teaspoon cream of tartar
- A pinch of salt

For Cream Cheese Filling:
- 4 packages cream cheese (8 ounce each)
- ¾ cup heavy whipping cream
- 1 tablespoon pure vanilla extract
- 1 ⅔ cups sugar
- 2 large eggs
- ¼ cup cornstarch

Directions

1. For Sponge Cake: Preheat your oven to 350 F & coat a large, springform pan generously with the butter.
2. Next, sift the cake flour with baking powder & salt in a medium sized mixing bowl until mixed well; set the mix aside.
3. Beat the egg yolks using an electric mixer in a large bowl for 3 minutes, on high power.
4. While the mixer still running, slowly add ⅓ cup of sugar & continue to beat for 5 more minutes, until thick light-yellow ribbons form in the bowl.
5. Beat in the lemon extracts and vanilla.

6. Sift the flour mixture on top of the batter & stir with hand until more white flecks appear.
7. Once done; immediately blend in the butter.
8. Now, beat the cream of tartar with egg whites using clean dry beaters in a clean bowl until completely frothy, on high.
9. Slowly add the leftover sugar & continue to beat until stiff peaks form.
10. Stir approximately ⅓ cup of the whites into the prepared batter, then gently fold in the leftover whites.
11. Gently spoon the prepared batter into the pan.
12. Bake the cake for 10 minutes, until the center just springs back. Let cool on a wire rack in the pan while you prepare the filling. Ensure that you don't remove the cake from your pan.

For Cream Cheese Filling:
1. Place 1 package of the cream cheese (8-ounce) with the cornstarch, and ⅓ cup of sugar in a large-sized mixing bowl.
2. Using an electric mixer; beat on low speed for 3 minutes, until creamy and then, beat in the leftover cream cheese.
3. Increase the speed of your mixer to high & beat in the leftover sugar and then, beat in the vanilla.
4. Slowly blend in the eggs, beating well after each addition.
5. Blend in the heavy cream. Ensure that you don't over-mix the prepared batter.
6. Gently spoon the cheese filling over the baked sponge cake layer.
7. Place the springform pan in a large shallow pan containing hot water that comes approximately 1" up the side of your pan.
8. Bake for an hour.
9. Let the cake to cool for 1 hour on a wire rack.
10. Using plastic wrap; cover the cake & refrigerate for overnight, until completely cold.
11. Remove the sides of springform pan. Slide the cake off the bottom of the pan onto a serving plate.
12. Leave the cake on the removable bottom of your pan & place it on a large serving plate

Lane Cake

Prep Time: 30 minutes
Cooking Time: 2 hours & 20 minutes
Servings: 12

Ingredients

For Cake
- 3 ½ cups cake flour (not self-rising)
- ½ pound unsalted butter, at room temperature
- 1½ teaspoons pure vanilla extract
- 8 large egg whites
- 1 cup whole milk
- A few drops of fresh lemon juice
- 1 tablespoon baking powder
- 2 cups granulated sugar
- 1 recipe Vanilla Milk Soak
- ½ teaspoon fine sea salt

For Frosting
- 1½ cups flaked coconut, sweetened
- 12 tablespoons unsalted butter
- 1½ cups pecans
- 12 egg yolks, large
- 1½ cups granulated sugar
- ½ cup brandy or bourbon
- 1½ cups golden raisins, finely chopped

For Vanilla Milk Soak
- 1 teaspoon pure vanilla extract
- ¼ cup whole milk

Directions

1. For Cake: Preheat your oven to 350F with the rack in middle. Butter three 9x2" round cake pans and then, line the bottoms with parchment; generously coat it with butter as well. Once done; dust the

pans lightly with flour, tapping the pans on the counter to shake any excess out.
2. Next, sift the flour with baking powder & salt in a large-sized mixing bowl until mixed well; set the mix aside.
3. Combine the milk with vanilla in a small bowl or large measuring cup; set the mix aside.
4. Cream the butter with sugar in the bowl of a stand mixer attached to the paddle for 3 to 5 minutes, until light & fluffy, on medium-high speed.
5. Decrease the speed to low & add the flour mixture in thirds, alternating with the milk mixture; starting and ending with the flour; continue to mix until just combined; scrapping down the sides and bottom of your bowl using a rubber spatula, as needed.
6. Wash & dry the mixer bowl; wipe the inside of your bowl with the lemon juice and ensure that the bowl is clean. Attach the bowl to the mixer stand & fit it with the whisk attachment.
7. Put the egg whites in a large mixing bowl or mixer bowl & beat for 2 to 3 minutes, until the whites hold soft peaks. Fold ¼ of egg whites into the cake batter to lighten it and then, gently fold in the leftover egg whites until incorporated well.
8. Evenly divide the prepared batter among the pans & smooth the tops using a large spatula.
9. Bake until a cake tester comes out clean, for 25 to 30 minutes. Let the cakes to cool for 15 minutes on a large wire rack, in the pans and then, invert onto a separate rack, peel the parchment off; turn the right side up to completely cool. Leave the oven on.
10. Meanwhile, prepare the frosting. Spread the pecans on a large-sized baking sheet & toast until toasted lightly & fragrant, for 5 minutes in the oven. Let cool and then, chop into ¼" pieces.
11. Now, over moderate heat in a medium-sized saucepan; heat the butter until melted. Remove from the heat & let cool. Once done; immediately whisk in the egg yolks and sugar until completely smooth.
12. Place the pan on moderate heat & cook until the frosting has thickened, stirring constantly using a large wooden spoon; don't bring the mix to a boil.
13. Remove from the heat; immediately add the toasted pecans, golden raisins, bourbon, and coconut, stirring well. Transfer the prepared frosting to a heatproof bowl & let cool.
14. For Vanilla Milk Soak: Combine the whole milk with vanilla extract in a large measuring cup.

15. To Assemble: Level the tops of two of the layers using a serrated knife to make them flat. Place one layer on a serving plate, cut side up. Brush the top with half of the prepared vanilla milk soak. Evenly spread the layer with ⅓ of frosting using a butter knife or an offset spatula. Place the second cake layer cut side up & brush with the leftover vanilla milk soak then spread with third of the frosting again. Place the final layer right side up on top & frost the top with the leftover frosting, leaving the sides of the cake naked.
16. Loosely cover & refrigerated for up to 5 days. Just before serving; bring it to room temperature and enjoy.

Hershey's Chocolate Cheesecake

Prep Time: 20 minutes
Cooking Time: 1 hour & 20 minutes
Servings: 08

Ingredients

- 1 can sweetened condensed milk (not evaporated milk) (14 oz)
- ¼ cup margarine or butter (approximately ½ stick)
- 3 packages cream cheese (8 ounces each), softened
- ½ cup Hershey's Cocoa
- 4 large eggs
- 1 tablespoon vanilla extract

Directions

1. Preheat your oven to 300F.
2. Microwave the butter in a medium-sized microwave-safe bowl until melted, for 30 to 45 seconds, at high power. Stir in the cocoa until completely smooth; set aside.
3. Beat the cream cheese in a large-sized mixing bowl. Add in the cocoa mixture & continue to beat. Slowly beat in the sweetened condensed milk until completely smooth. Add vanilla and eggs & beat well. Pour the prepared batter into the pan.
4. Bake until set, for 65 minutes. Remove the pan carefully from the oven to wire rack; loosen the cake from side of your pan. Let completely cool; remove the side of your pan. Garnish per your likings. Cover & refrigerate any leftover cheesecake.

New York Cheesecake

Prep Time: 10 minutes
Cooking Time: 1 hour & 30 minutes
Servings: 12

Ingredients

For Crust
- 140g digestive biscuits, made into fine crumbs (add 2 additional biscuits, if needed)
- 1 tablespoon golden caster, or granulated sugar
- 85g butter, plus additional for tin

For Cheesecake Filling
- 900g Philadelphia cheese, or any of your favorite full-fat cheese, soft
- 3 tablespoons plain flour
- 1 ½ teaspoons vanilla extract
- 3 large eggs, plus 1 yolk
- 1 ½ teaspoons lemon juice
- 284ml carton soured cream
- Zest of 1 lemon, finely grated
- 250g golden caster sugar

For Soured Cream Topping:
- 2 teaspoons fresh lemon juice
- 1 tablespoon golden caster sugar
- 142ml carton soured cream

Directions

1. Preheat your oven to 350F with an oven shelf in middle. Line the base of a 23cm springform cake tin by putting a square piece of foil or parchment paper over the tin base and then, clipping the side on so the foil or paper is trapped & any excess sticks out of the bottom.
2. For Crust: Over moderate heat in a medium pan; heat 85g of butter until melted. Stir in 1 tablespoon of granulated or golden caster sugar & 140g of digestive biscuit crumbs so the mixture is moistened evenly.
3. Press the mixture into the bottom of your pan & bake in the preheated oven for 10 minutes. Let cool on the wire rack while you prepare the filling.
4. For Filling: Increase your oven's temperature to 450 F. Beat 900g full-fat soft cheese in a tabletop mixer attached to the paddle for 2 minutes, until completely creamy, at medium-low speed.
5. With the mixer still running on low, slowly add 250g of golden caster sugar and then 3 tablespoons of plain flour and a pinch of salt, scraping down the paddle and the sides of your bowl twice.
6. Swap the paddle attachment for the whisk. Continue to add 1½ teaspoons vanilla extract with 2 teaspoons lemon zest & 1 ½ teaspoons lemon juice. Slowly whisk in 1 yolk and 3 large eggs; scraping the bowl & whisk at least twice.
7. Stir a 284ml carton of soured cream until completely smooth, then measure 200ml. Continue low speed as you add the measured soured cream (set the remaining aside). Whisk to blend but ensure that you don't over-beat.
8. Brush the sides of your springform tin with the melted butter & put on the baking sheet. Pour in the filling & bake for 10 minutes.
9. Reduce your oven's temperature to 220 F & bake for 45 more minutes.
10. Turn the oven off & open the oven door for a cheesecake. Let cool for 2 hours in the oven.
11. Combine the kept-aside soured cream with a 142ml carton of the soured cream, 2 teaspoons lemon juice & 1 tablespoon golden caster sugar for the topping. Spread on top of the cheesecake and the edges. Loosely cover with aluminum foil & refrigerate for overnight.
12. Run a round-bladed knife around the sides of the tin to loosen any stuck edges. Unlock the side, slide the cheesecake off the bottom of the tin onto a plate, then slide the parchment paper out from underneath.

Smith Island Cake

Prep Time: 50 minutes
Cooking Time: 50 minutes
Servings: 16

Ingredients

For Cake:
- 5 large eggs, at room temperature
- 1 ½ cups softened salted butter, at room temperature
- 2 cups white sugar
- cooking spray
- 2 teaspoons vanilla extract
- 1 ½ teaspoons baking powder
- 3 ¾ cups all-purpose flour, sifted
- ¾ teaspoon baking soda
- 1 ¾ cups buttermilk, at room temperature
- ½ teaspoon kosher salt

For Icing:
- 24 ounces bittersweet baking chocolate, chopped
- ¼ cup light corn syrup
- 4 cups heavy cream
- ¼ teaspoon kosher salt

Directions

1. For Icing: Combine the corn syrup with cream over moderate heat in a medium-sized saucepan; bring the mix just to a simmer, stirring now and then. Once done; immediately remove it from the heat.
2. Next, pour the hot cream mixture carefully on top of the chocolate in a large microwave-safe bowl and sprinkle with salt. Let stand for a couple of minutes. Whisk until completely smooth & let cool for an hour, to room temperature. Let the icing to chill in the refrigerator for 45 minutes, until spreadable and thickened; stirring halfway.
3. In the meantime, prepare the cake layers. Preheat your oven to 350F. Coat nine 8 ½" round disposable cake pans with the cooking spray. Line the bottoms with parchment paper & gently spray with a bit of cooking spray.

4. Beat butter in a stand mixer attached to the paddle for a minute or two, until smooth & creamy, at medium speed. Slowly add sugar & continue to beat for 3 more minutes, until light & fluffy. Slowly add the eggs & beat after each addition until just incorporated. Beat in the vanilla.
5. Whisk the flour with baking soda, baking powder & salt in a medium-sized mixing bowl. Work in 3 batches; add flour mixture to the butter mixture alternately with buttermilk, beginning & ending with the flour mixture & beat on medium speed.
6. Evenly divide the prepared batter (approximately 1 cup each) among the prepared pans & smooth using an offset spatula. Work in batches & bake for 12 to 14 minutes, until a wooden pick comes out clean. Let cool for 10 minutes in the pans on wire rack. Turn out the cakes onto the wire racks to completely cool.
7. Place 1 cake layer on a large round cake board & spread with approximately ⅓ cup of the icing using a small offset spatula. Top with one more cake layer & spread with ⅓ cup of more icing. Repeat the process with the leftover icing & layers. Coat the top & sides of your cake with a thin layer of icing. Let the cake to chill for an hour, reserving the leftover icing.
8. Place the chilled cake over a rimmed baking pan on a wire rack. Microwave the kept-aside icing in 30-second intervals until smooth and pourable, at medium (50%) power, stirring after each one. Pour the prepared icing in a slow, steady stream on top of the cake, starting at the center and moving to the outer edges. Smooth the sides out & fill any gaps using an offset spatula.
9. Let the cake to chill for an hour, until set. Carefully transfer the cake to a large serving plate. Serve at room temperature. Enjoy.

Texas Sheet Cake

Prep Time: 30 minutes
Cooking Time: 20 minutes
Servings: 32

Ingredients

For Cake:
- 2 cups all-purpose flour
- 1 cup butter
- 2 cups white sugar
- ½ cup sour cream
- 1 cup water
- 2 large eggs
- 1 teaspoon baking soda
- 5 tablespoons unsweetened cocoa powder
- ½ teaspoon salt

For Icing:
- 6 tablespoons milk
- ½ cup butter
- 1 teaspoon vanilla extract
- 5 tablespoons cocoa powder, unsweetened
- 1 cup walnuts, chopped
- 4 cups confectioners' sugar

Directions

1. Grease & flour a large jelly roll pan and then, preheat your oven to 350F.
2. For Cake: Combine the flour with baking soda, sugar, and salt in a large-sized mixing bowl until mixed well. Beat in the eggs and sour cream.
3. Next, over low heat in a large saucepan; heat the butter until melted. Stir in cocoa powder and water. Bring the mix to a boil and then, remove from the heat. Let slightly cool and then, stir the cocoa mix into the flour-egg mix until blended well. Pour the prepared batter into the pan.
4. Bake for 20 minutes, until a toothpick comes out clean.
5. Meanwhile, prepare the icing. Combine the milk with butter, and cocoa powder over moderate heat in a large saucepan. Bring this mix to a boil and then, remove from the heat. Stir in the vanilla and confectioners' sugar, then fold in the walnuts; continue to mix until blended well.
6. Spread this prepared icing on top of the warm cake. Enjoy.

Tunnel of Fudge Cake

Prep Time: 20 minutes
Cooking Time: 1 hour & 10 minutes
Servings: 16

Ingredients

For Cake:
- 2 cups all-purpose flour
- 1 ½ cups unsalted butter, at room temperature
- 2 boxes Chocolate Fudge Frosting Mix
- 6 large eggs, at room temperature
- 2 cups walnuts, chopped
- 1 ½ cups sugar

For Glaze:
- 4 to 6 teaspoons milk
- ¼ cup unsweetened cocoa powder
- ¾ cup confectioners' sugar

Directions

1. Coat a 12-cup Bundt pan generously with butter and then, preheat your oven to 350F.
2. Next, whisk the flour with frosting mix in a medium-sized mixing bowl until mixed well and then, stir in the walnuts; set the mix aside.
3. Cream the butter in the bowl of a stand mixer attached to the paddle for 3 to 5 minutes, until lighter in color & fluffy, on medium speed. Slowly add the eggs; beat for half a minute after each addition. Stop often & scrape the sides of your bowl, as needed. With the mixer still running at medium speed, slowly stream in the sugar. Once added completely, continue beating for 3 more minutes, at medium speed. Remove the bowl from your mixer & fold in the flour-frosting-nut mix using a Silicone spatula until no streaks of flour are present. Fill the prepared pan with batter.
4. Bake until the top is just set, for 55 to 60 minutes; ensure that you don't over-bake.
5. Let the cake to cool for 2 hours in the pan set on a rack and then, remove the cake from your pan to completely cool.

For Glaze:
1. Whisk the cocoa powder with confectioners' sugar, and milk in a small-sized mixing bowl. Start with the smaller quantity of milk; add more if required until you reach your desired level of consistency.
2. Drizzle the glaze on top of the cooled cake. Let sit for a couple of minutes & let the glaze to harden. Serve and enjoy.

Strawberry Shortcake

Prep Time: 20 minutes
Cooking Time: 30 minutes
Servings: 06

Ingredients

- 5 tablespoons sugar
- 1 ½ pounds strawberries, stemmed & quartered
- 2 cups all-purpose flour
- 1 ½ cups heavy cream
- 2 teaspoons baking powder
- ¼ teaspoon baking soda
- 2 tablespoons sugar
- Whipped Cream, as needed
- ¾ teaspoon salt

Whipped Cream:
- 1 ½ teaspoons vanilla extract
- 3 tablespoons sugar
- 1 ½ cups chilled heavy cream
- 1 teaspoon lemon zest, freshly grated

Directions

1. Combine strawberries with sugar & refrigerate for half an hour.
2. Next, preheat your oven to 400F.
3. Sift the flour with baking soda, baking powder, leftover sugar & salt in a medium-sized mixing bowl.
4. Add in the heavy cream & continue to mix until just mixed. Place the prepared mixture in an ungreased, large square pan & bake for 18 to 20 minutes, until turns golden.
5. Remove the shortcake from pan & place on a wire rack to slightly cool. Evenly cut into six pieces & split each piece horizontally in half.
6. Spoon a bit of the strawberries with their juice onto each shortcake bottom. Top with a generous dollop of whipped cream and then the shortcake top. Spoon some more strawberries on top & serve.

For Whipped Cream:
1. Beat the heavy cream with sugar, lemon zest, and vanilla using a mixer for 1 ½ to 2 minutes, until soft peaks form.

Pies

Apple Pie

Prep Time: 20 minutes
Cooking Time: 1 hour & 20 minutes
Servings: 08

Ingredients

- 6 to 7 cups tart apples, peeled & thinly sliced
- Dough for double-crust pie
- ⅓ cup brown sugar, packed
- 1 teaspoon ground cinnamon
- ¼ teaspoon ground nutmeg
- 1 tablespoon fresh lemon juice
- ¼ cup all-purpose flour
- 1 tablespoon butter
- ¼ teaspoon ground ginger
- 1 egg white, large
- ⅓ cup sugar

Optional Ingredients:
- Ground cinnamon
- Coarse or turbinado sugar
- Caramel sauce
- Vanilla bean ice cream

Directions

1. Preheat your oven to 375F.
2. Next, roll half of the dough on a lightly floured surface into a ⅛" thick circle; transfer to a 9" pie plate. Chill while you prepare the filling. Combine the flour with sugars and spices in a small-sized mixing bowl until mixed well. Toss the apples with the fresh lemon juice in a large-sized mixing bowl. Add in the sugar mixture; gently toss to coat. Add filling to the crust and dot with the butter.
3. Roll the leftover dough into ⅛" thick circle. Place on top of the filling. Trim, seal & flute the edge. Cut slits in top. Beat the egg white until completely foamy; brush on top of the crust and sprinkle with the ground cinnamon and turbinado sugar.
4. Bake until crust is golden brown, and filling is bubbly, for 60 to 70 minutes, on the lowest rack. Feel free to cover the same using an aluminum foil halfway if the crust starts to get too dark. Let cool on the wire rack. Serve with caramel sauce and ice cream, if desired.

Black Bottom Pie

Prep Time: 20 minutes
Cooking Time: 2 hours & 10 minutes
Servings: 08

Ingredients

- Pie crust (homemade or store bought)
- ¼ cup heavy cream
- 4 ounces bittersweet chocolate, chopped
- 1 ½ cups old fashioned or quick Quaker® Oats, uncooked
- ¾ cup packed light brown sugar
- 1 teaspoon vanilla extract
- 5 tablespoons unsalted butter, melted
- 1 cup dark corn syrup
- 4 eggs, large
- ½ teaspoon kosher salt

Directions

1. Preheat your oven to 350 F with a rack in middle. Toast the oats for 5 minutes on a large baking sheet; give it a good stir & put in the oven again to toast for 5 more minutes. Set aside to cool. Decrease your oven's temperature to 325 F.
2. For Chocolate Layer: Bring the heavy cream to a boil over moderate heat in a large saucepan. Once done; remove it from the heat & add the pieces of chocolate. Thoroughly mix and ensure that the ingredients are evenly combined; let sit for a couple of minutes.
3. Pour the prepared chocolate mixture on top of the pie crust & evenly spread; put the pie crust in the freezer until hardened.
4. Next, mix the brown sugar with melted butter, and salt in a large-sized mixing bowl. Add the corn syrup, and vanilla; whisk until mixed well. Slowly add the eggs; thoroughly mix after each addition. Now, stir in the previously toasted cooled oats.
5. Remove the pie crust from your freezer & place on the baking sheet. Pour in the prepared filling. Place the pie in the oven & bake for 50 minutes, on middle rack.
6. Let the pie to cool on a wire rack roughly for 2 hours. Serve with whipped cream & enjoy.

Blueberry Pie

Prep Time: 20 minutes
Cooking Time: 50 minutes
Servings: 08

Ingredients

- 4 cups blueberries, fresh
- ¾ cup white sugar
- 1 package double-crust pie pastry (14.1 ounce), thawed
- ½ teaspoon ground cinnamon
- 3 tablespoons cornstarch
- 1 tablespoon butter
- ¼ teaspoon salt

Directions

1. Preheat your oven to 375 F with the rack in the lowest position.
2. Next, combine the cornstarch with cinnamon, sugar, and salt in a large-sized mixing bowl until mixed well. Sprinkle the blueberries with this mix.
3. Line a pie dish with one of the pie crusts. Pour the berry mixture into the crust & dot with the butter. Cut the leftover pastry into ½ to ¾" wide strips. Weave a lattice top using the strips. Crimp & flute the edges.
4. Bake for 50 minutes, until filling turns bubbly & crust turns golden brown.

Bumbleberry Pie

Prep Time: 20 minutes
Cooking Time: 1 hour & 30 minutes
Servings: 08

Ingredients

- 1 cup cold butter
- 1 ½ cups all-purpose flour
- 1 teaspoon sugar
- ¼ cup cold water
- 1 teaspoon salt

For Filling:
- 1 cup fresh or frozen rhubarb, diced & thawed
- 1 medium tart apple, peeled and diced
- 1 cup fresh or frozen raspberries, thawed and drained
- ½ cup all-purpose flour
- 1 cup fresh or frozen strawberries, sliced, thawed & drained
- 1 tablespoon fresh lemon juice
- 1 cup sugar

Directions

1. Mix the flour, sugar, and salt in a small-sized mixing bowl until mixed well. Cut in the butter until you get coarse crumbs like mixture. Slowly add the water, gently tossing with a fork until a ball forms. Cover & refrigerate until easy to handle, for an hour.
2. Preheat your oven to 400F. Roll half of the dough out to fit a 9" pie plate on a lightly floured surface. Transfer the crust to pie plate; trim to ½" beyond the edge of your plate.
3. Combine all the filling ingredients together in a large-sized mixing bowl and immediately pour into the prepared crust.
4. Roll the leftover dough out; cut decorative shapes out using a cookie cutter. Place on top of the filling. Loosely cover the edge using aluminum foil.
5. Bake in the preheated oven for 20 minutes. Decrease the temperature to 350 F; remove the foil as well. Bake until crust is golden brown, and filling is bubbly, for 40 to 45 minutes or. Let cool on the wire rack to completely cool.

Cherry Pie

Prep Time: 40 minutes
Cooking Time: 1 hour & 20 minutes
Servings: 08

Ingredients

- 4 tablespoons cornstarch
- 1 to 1 ½ cups granulated sugar
- 4 cups tart cherries; fresh or frozen
- ⅛ tablespoon almond extract
- Pie crust or pie dough recipe for 2 crust pie
- 1 tablespoon granulated sugar
- 1 ½ tablespoons butter

Directions

1. Place cherries over moderate heat in a medium-sized saucepan. Cover and cook for a couple of minutes, until the cherries lose considerable juice. Once done, immediately remove it from the heat. Next, mix the cornstarch with sugar in a small-sized mixing bowl until mixed well. Pour this mix into the hot cherries & mix well. Add the almond extract & mix well. Place the mixture on low heat again & cook until thickened, stirring now and then. Remove from the heat & let cool. Feel free to add a bit of water; if the filling is too thick or add a bit of more cornstarch, if the mixture appears to be too thin.
2. Preheat your oven to 375F.
3. Prepare your crust, dividing it into half. Roll each piece of large enough out to fit into an 8 to 9" pan. Pour the cooled cherry mixture into the crust and then, dot with the butter. Moisten the edge of bottom crust. Place top crust on & flute the edge of the pie. Make a slit in middle of the crust for steam to escape and then, sprinkle with the sugar.
4. Bake for 50 minutes. Remove from the oven & place on a rack to cool.

Chiffon Pie

Prep Time: 35 minutes
Cooking Time: 30 minutes
Servings: 12

Ingredients

- 1 prepared graham cracker crust (9")
- ¼ cup cold water
- 1 package unflavored gelatin (.25 ounce)
- 4 large egg yolks
- 1 cup white sugar, divided
- ½ cup lemon juice, fresh
- 1 teaspoon lemon zest
- 4 egg whites
- ½ teaspoon salt

Directions

1. Fill a large bowl with cold water; add the gelatin & let stand for 5 minutes, until softened.
2. Beat the egg yolks with ½ cup of sugar, salt, and lemon juice in a large bowl until completely smooth. Cook in the top of a double boiler until you get custard like consistency, stirring constantly. Add the softened gelatin and grated lemon zest; thoroughly stir & set the mix aside for 10 to 15 minutes, until thickened & cool.
3. Beat the egg whites in a ceramic, metal, or glass bowl until completely foamy. Slowly add the leftover sugar; continue to beat until soft peaks form; fold the egg whites into the cooled custard mixture.
4. Fill the prepared pie shell with the filling & let chill in a refrigerator for 2 hours, until firm. Just before serving; garnish with the sweetened whipped cream. Enjoy.

Coconut Custard Pie

Prep Time: 20 minutes
Cooking Time: 40 minutes
Servings: 08

Ingredients

- 1 tablespoon flaked coconut
- 1 ½ cups white sugar
- 1 cup milk
- ½ cup butter
- 1 cup flaked coconut
- 2 large eggs
- 1 unbaked pie crust (9")
- 2 tablespoons all-purpose flour
- 1 teaspoon vanilla extract

Directions

1. Preheat your oven to 350F.
2. Next, beat the butter with eggs, and sugar using an electric mixer in a large bowl, on low speed. Blend in the flour. Slowly mix in the milk. Add 1 cup of coconut flakes & vanilla; continue to mix the ingredients.
3. Fill the unbaked pie crust with the prepared filling. Sprinkle with 1 tablespoon of the coconut flakes.
4. Bake for 40 to 50 minutes, until filling is set. Serve and enjoy.

Derby Pie

Prep Time: 20 minutes
Cooking Time: 50 minutes
Servings: 08

Ingredients

- 1 pie crust pastry (9")
- 4 large eggs
- 1 cup light corn syrup
- 1 ¼ cups chocolate chips
- 1 cup white sugar
- ½ cup melted butter
- 1 teaspoon vanilla extract
- 2 tablespoons bourbon, optional
- 1 cup pecans, chopped

Directions

1. Press the pie crust into a 9" pie plate and then, preheat your oven to 350F.
2. Beat the corn syrup with eggs, and white sugar using an electric mixer in a bowl until blended well, on low speed; stir in the pecans, chocolate chips, butter, vanilla extract, and bourbon.
3. Fill the prepared pie crust with the prepared mix.
4. Bake for 45 to 50 minutes, until set.

Grape Pie

Prep Time: 20 minutes
Cooking Time: 50 minutes
Servings: 08

Ingredients

- 5 cups grapes
- 1 package double-crust pie pastry (14.1 ounce), thawed
- ¼ cup all-purpose flour
- 1 ¼ cups white sugar
- ¾ teaspoon lemon juice
- 1 ½ tablespoons unsalted butter, cut into small pieces
- A pinch of salt

Directions

1. Preheat your oven to 400F with a sheet pan on the lower rack. Press one pie pastry into a large pie pan; set second pastry aside.
2. Wash & stem the grapes; squeeze the grape pulp out of the skins into a large saucepan. Place skins into a large bowl & set aside.
3. Mash a few grapes in the saucepan until they release their juices. Bring it to a boil, over medium-low heat.
4. Remove the seeds by running the hot pulp mixture through a food mill. Add pulp to the skins in the large bowl & immediately stir in the lemon juice.
5. Next, combine the flour with sugar, and salt in a separate bowl; stir into the grape mixture & pour into the bottom pastry. Dot with the butter & cover with the second pastry. Flute the edges & cut little slits in the top crust for steam to escape.
6. Place the pie on the baking sheet in the preheated oven; bake for 45 to 50 minutes, until crust is golden brown. Let completely cool before serving.

Jelly Cream Pie

Prep Time: 20 minutes
Cooking Time: 40 minutes
Servings: 08

Ingredients

For White Cake Cookies:
- 2 large eggs, at room temperature
- 1 box white cake mix (15.25 oz)
- ⅓ cup vegetable oil

For Cream Cheese Filling:
- 8 ounces cream cheese, room temperature
- ½ cup unsalted butter, room temperature
- 1 teaspoon vanilla
- 3 ½ cups confectioner's powdered sugar

Additional Ingredients:
- 10 ounces milk chocolate candy melts
- 4 tablespoons strawberry jam

Directions

1. Preheat your oven to 350F.
2. Next, combine the eggs with cake mix, and oil. Scoop heaping tablespoons out & roll them into small balls. Slightly flatten the dough using your palms & place on a silicone baking mat or a parchment paper lined cookie sheet.
3. Bake until the bottoms turn slightly golden, for 8 to 10 minutes. Let completely cool.
4. For Cream Cheese Filling: Combine the cream cheese with butter using an electric mixer.
5. Slowly add the powdered sugar, mixing well between each addition; stopping and scrapping the sides down, as required.
6. Mix in the vanilla.
7. Transfer the prepared filling to a large piping bag & set aside.
8. To Assemble: Pipe a dam around top of a cookie using cream cheese filling. Spoon approximately ½ tablespoon of the jam into middle. Place another cookie over the filling, upside down (flat side up).
9. Repeat with the leftover cookies. Freeze all assembled cookies for 10 minutes.
10. Heat the chocolate melting candy per the directions mentioned on the package until melted.
11. Place the cookies on a cooling rack & place rack over a parchment paper or silicone mat.
12. Spoon approximately 2 tablespoons of the melted chocolate over each cookie & let the chocolate run over sides. It should cool & harden quickly.

Huckleberry Pie

Prep Time: 20 minutes
Cooking Time: 40 minutes
Servings: 08

Ingredients

- 2 teaspoons white sugar
- 1 recipe pastry for a 9" double crust pie
- 2 tablespoons heavy cream
- 4 cups huckleberries
- ¾ cup white sugar
- 2 tablespoons butter
- 1 tablespoon all-purpose flour
- 2 tablespoons fresh lemon juice
- 1 teaspoon lemon zest, grated

Directions

1. Preheat your oven to 425F.
2. Place the huckleberries in a pan lined with pastry. Next, mix ¾ cup of sugar with flour in a small-sized mixing bowl. Evenly spoon on top of the berries. Sprinkle lemon juice and lemon rind on top.
3. Dot with the butter. Cover with the top crust. Seal the edges & cut the steam vents in top. Brush the surface with cream, avoiding the fluted edges of crust and then, sprinkle with approximately 2 teaspoons of sugar.
4. Bake for 15 minutes. Decrease the heat of your oven to 350 F & bake until the crust turns golden brown, for 20 to 25 more minutes.

Lemon Chiffon Pie

Prep Time: 20 minutes
Cooking Time: 20 minutes
Servings: 12

Ingredients

- 1 package unflavored gelatin (.25 ounce)
- ¼ cup cold water
- 1 cup white sugar, divided
- 4 large egg yolks
- 1 teaspoon lemon zest
- ½ cup fresh lemon juice
- 4 large egg whites
- 1 prepared graham cracker crust (9")
- ½ teaspoon salt

Directions

1. Fill a large bowl with cold water; add the gelatin & let stand for 5 minutes, until softened.
2. Beat the egg yolks with ½ cup of sugar, salt, and lemon juice in a large bowl until completely smooth. Cook in the top of a double boiler until you get custard like consistency, stirring constantly. Add the softened gelatin and grated lemon zest; thoroughly stir & set the mix aside for 10 to 15 minutes, until thickened & cool.
3. Beat the egg whites in a glass, ceramic, or metal bowl until completely foamy. Slowly add the leftover sugar, continue beating until soft peaks form; fold the egg whites into the cooled custard mixture.
4. Fill the prepared pie shell with filling & let chill in a refrigerator for 2 hours, until firm. Garnish with sweetened whipped cream. Serve and enjoy.

Mississippi Mud Pie

Prep Time: 20 minutes
Cooking Time: 60 minutes
Servings: 10

Ingredients

- 2 packs crème filled chocolate biscuits (154g each,) centers scraped out
- 100g melted butter

For Brownie Layer
- 25g plain flour
- 100g butter
- 140g dark soft brown sugar
- 2 medium eggs
- 140g dark chocolate, chopped, plus extra for grating

For Chocolate Custard Layer
- ½ teaspoon vanilla extract
- 500g pot ready-made vanilla custard
- 3 gelatin sheets
- 50g dark chocolate

For Topping
- 300ml double cream

Directions

1. Preheat your oven to 350F. Whizz the biscuits to a fine crumb in a food processor. Pour in the melted butter; briefly pulse to mix well. Spoon into a 24cm pie dish & press into the base and up the sides. Bake until firm up, for 10 minutes.
2. For Brownie Layer: Heat the butter & chocolate in a bowl set over a pan of simmering water until melted.
3. Whisk the eggs in a separate bowl until pale, fluffy & doubled in size. Once done; add the sugar & whisk for a minute or two, until thickened. Fold in the chocolate mixture; sieve in the flour & fold in.
4. Pour into the baked biscuit case & return to the oven until the brownie has a crust on top, for 15 to 20 minutes. Set aside & leave to cool.
5. Once done, put the custard, vanilla, and chocolate in a large pan & cook until the chocolate has melted into the custard, over a medium heat, stirring. Remove from the heat.
6. Soak the gelatin in a bit of cold water & remove from the water once softened; squeeze to remove any excess. Stir into the warm custard mixture until completely dissolved. Let the custard to slightly cool and then, pour on top of the brownie layer. Put in the fridge for a couple of hours.
7. Remove the mud pie from fridge half an hour prior to serving. Just before serving, whip the cream to soft peaks and spoon it over the custard layer, then grate over a bit of dark chocolate.

Pecan Pie

Prep Time: 30 minutes
Cooking Time: 50 minutes
Servings: 08

Ingredients

- 1 ¾ cups white sugar
- 3 large eggs
- 1 unbaked pie shell (9")
- ¼ cup dark corn syrup
- 2 teaspoons cornstarch
- 1 teaspoon vanilla extract
- ¼ cup butter
- 1 tablespoon cold water
- 1 ¼ cups pecans, chopped
- ¼ teaspoon salt

Directions

1. Preheat your oven to 350F.
2. Combine the corn syrup with sugar, butter, cornstarch, and water over moderate heat in a large saucepan; bring the mix to a boil and then, remove from the heat.
3. Next, beat the eggs in a large bowl until completely frothy. Slowly beat in the cooked syrup mixture. Stir in pecans, vanilla, and salt.
4. Pour the pecan mixture into the pie shell. Bake for 45 to 50 minutes, until filling is set.

Rhubarb Pie

Prep Time: 30 minutes
Cooking Time: 1 hour & 20 minutes
Servings: 08

Ingredients

- 1 package double-crust pie pastry (14.1 ounce), thawed
- 6 tablespoons all-purpose flour
- 1 tablespoon butter
- 4 cups rhubarb, chopped
- 1 ⅓ cups white sugar

Directions

1. Preheat your oven to 450F with an oven rack in the lowest position.
2. Next, line the sides and bottom of a large pie plate with one pie crust. Combine flour with sugar in a large bowl and then, sprinkle the prepared bottom crust with ¼ of sugar mixture.
3. Heap rhubarb on top & sprinkle with the leftover sugar mixture. Dot with butter & cover with the top crust.
4. Bake for 15 minutes. Decrease your oven's temperature to 350 F & continue to bake for 40 to 45 minutes, until crust is golden brown, and filling is bubbly. Serve warm or cold. Enjoy.

Shoofly Pie

Prep Time: 20 minutes
Cooking Time: 70 minutes
Servings: 08

Ingredients

- Dough for single-crust pie
- 1 large egg yolk, room temperature, lightly beaten
- ½ cup brown sugar, packed
- 1 large egg, room temperature
- ½ cup molasses
- 1 ½ teaspoons all-purpose flour
- ½ teaspoon baking soda
- 1 cup boiling water

For Topping:
- ¾ cup brown sugar, packed
- 1 ½ cups all-purpose flour
- ¾ teaspoon baking soda
- 6 tablespoons cold butter, cubed
- A dash of salt

Directions

1. Roll the dough out to fit a 9" deep-dish pie plate on a floured surface. Trim & flute the edge. Refrigerate for half an hour.
2. In the meantime, preheat your oven to 425F.
3. For Filling: Combine the molasses with brown sugar, flour, egg, and baking soda. Slowly stir in the boiling water & let completely cool.
4. Line crust with foil. Once done; fill with the pie weights, uncooked rice, or dried beans. Bake for 15 minutes on a lower oven rack.
5. Remove the foil & pie weights; brush the crust lightly with the egg yolk and continue to bake for 5 more minutes. Let cool on the wire rack. Decrease your oven's temperature to 350 F.
6. Whisk the topping ingredients (except cold butter) in a separate bowl. Cut in the butter until completely crumbly. Add filling to the crust and then, sprinkle with the topping. Cover the edge of pie with aluminum foil. Bake for 45 to 50 minutes, until filling turns golden brown and is set. Let cool on a wire rack and then, store in a refrigerator.

Strawberry Rhubarb Pie

Prep Time: 30 minutes
Cooking Time: 40 minutes
Servings: 08

Ingredients

- 1 recipe pastry for a 9" double crust pie
- 2 pints strawberries, hulled and quartered
- 1-pound rhubarb, cut into ¼" slices
- 2 tablespoons butter
- ½ cup all-purpose flour
- 1 egg yolk, large
- 2 tablespoons white sugar
- 1 cup white sugar

Directions

1. Preheat your oven to 400F.
2. Next, mix the flour with sugar in a large-sized mixing bowl until mixed well.
3. Add chopped rhubarb and strawberries. Gently toss with flour and sugar; let stand for half an hour.
4. Pour filling into the prepared pie crust. Dot the top with butter & cover with the top crust. Seal the edges of top & bottom crust lightly with water.
5. Apply yolk over the pie using a pastry brush and then, sprinkle with the sugar.
6. Cut small holes in top to let steam escape.
7. Bake until bubbly and brown, for 35 to 40 minutes. Let cool on the rack.

Sweet Potato Pie

Prep Time: 40 minutes
Cooking Time: 50 minutes
Servings: 08

Ingredients

- ⅓ cup softened butter, at room temperature
- Dough for single-crust pie
- ½ teaspoon ground nutmeg
- ¾ cup evaporated milk
- 2 medium sweet potatoes (approximately 1 ½ pounds), peeled & cubed
- ½ cup sugar
- 2 lightly beaten eggs, large, at room temperature
- ½ teaspoon ground cinnamon
- 1 teaspoon vanilla extract
- ¼ teaspoon salt

Directions

1. Preheat your oven to 425F.
2. Roll the dough to approximately ⅛" thick circle on a lightly floured surface, transfer to a large pie plate. Trim the crust to ½" beyond the rim of your plate; flute the edge. Refrigerate while you prepare the filling.
3. Place the sweet potatoes in a medium-sized saucepan; add water (enough to cover) and bring it to a boil, over moderate heat. Once done; decrease the heat & cook for 13 to 15 minutes, until tender, uncovered. Drain the potatoes; return to the pan. Mash until smooth; let cool to room temperature.
4. Next, cream the butter with sugar in a bowl. Add eggs & mix well. Add milk followed by 2 cups mashed sweet potatoes, cinnamon, vanilla, nutmeg, and salt; continue to mix the ingredients until mixed well. Pour into the crust. Bake for 12 to 15 minutes. Decrease the heat to 350 F & bake for 35 to 40 minutes, until set or a knife comes out clean. Let cool on a wire rack & refrigerate any leftovers.

Pudding

Butter Scotch Pudding

Prep Time: 20 minutes
Cooking Time: 30 minutes
Servings: 04 cups

Ingredients

- 2 cups whole milk, divided
- 1 cup heavy cream
- 3 tablespoons cornstarch
- 1 cup dark brown sugar
- 3 large egg yolks
- 1 teaspoon vanilla extract
- 2 tablespoons unsalted butter
- A pinch of salt

Directions

1. Whisk the cornstarch with ¼ cup of milk in a small-sized mixing bowl until mixed well. Set the mix aside.
2. Next, whisk the leftover milk with cream, sugar, and salt over moderate heat in a medium-sized saucepan. Cook until it's steaming but don't bring it to a boil.
3. Meanwhile, whisk the egg yolks in a separate small bowl. Once the milk is steaming, slowly stream in approximately ½ cup of hot milk mix into the egg yolks; continue to whisk the ingredients.
4. Slowly add the egg yolk mixture into the pot again, followed by the cornstarch mixture. Continue cooking until the mixture has thickened & begins to simmer, over medium heat, whisking constantly.
5. Remove from the heat & immediately whisk in the butter followed by the vanilla.
6. Pour into individual serving dishes. Top each dish with a layer of plastic wrap touching the top of the pudding to prevent a skin from forming; let chill for a couple of hours before serving. Top with the whipped cream.

Hasty Pudding

Prep Time: 40 minutes
Cooking Time: 1 hour & 30 minutes
Servings: 10

Ingredients

- ½ cup all-purpose flour
- 3 cups coarse stone-ground yellow cornmeal
- 1 tablespoon ground cinnamon
- ½ cup maple syrup
- 8 cups half-and-half
- ½ cup molasses
- 4 tablespoons unsalted butter (approximately ½ stick), cut into pieces
- ½ cup light brown sugar, packed
- Juice & zest of 1 orange, fresh
- 2 teaspoons salt

Whipped Cream:
- ⅓ cup confectioners' sugar
- 2 cups heavy whipping cream

Directions

1. Preheat your oven to 325 F with a rack in middle. Butter a large baking dish.
2. Next, whisk the flour with cornmeal, cinnamon, and salt in a large bowl until mixed well; set the mix aside.
3. Whisk the half-and-half with maple syrup, brown sugar, and molasses over moderate heat in a large saucepan. Heat until just begins to boil. Once done; decrease the heat to a simmer & slowly add the cornmeal mixture, whisking constantly. Let simmer & whisk for 5 minutes. Whisk in the orange zest and juice and the butter.
4. Transfer the prepared pudding to the baking dish & bake for 1 hour 15 minutes, until set. Remove & let cool for a couple of minutes. Serve topped with the whipped cream, evenly spread on top of the pudding.

Whipped Cream:
1. Whip the cream using an electric mixer until soft peaks form.
2. Add the confectioners' sugar & continue to whip until the cream holds stiff peaks. Refrigerate until needed.

Persimmon Pudding

Prep Time: 30 minutes
Cooking Time: 55 minutes
Servings: 08

Ingredients

- 2 cups all-purpose flour
- ½ teaspoon baking soda
- 2 teaspoons baking powder
- 2 ½ cups white sugar
- 2 beaten eggs, large
- ½ teaspoon ground cinnamon
- 2 ½ cups milk
- ¼ teaspoon vanilla extract
- 2 cups persimmon pulp
- 4 tablespoons butter, melted
- A pinch of salt

Directions

1. Grease a large baking dish and then, preheat your oven to 325F.
2. Next, combine the persimmon pulp with sugar, baking soda, and eggs in a large-sized mixing bowl until mixed well.
3. Add the flour, baking powder, vanilla, cinnamon, and salt. Pour in the melted butter and milk; give it a good stir to combine.
4. Pour the mix into the prepared baking pan & bake for 55 minutes.

Tapioca Pudding

Prep Time: 20 minutes
Cooking Time: 20 minutes
Servings: 06

Ingredients

- ½ teaspoon vanilla extract
- 3 cups whole milk
- ½ cup quick-cooking tapioca
- 2 beaten eggs, large
- ½ cup white sugar
- ¼ teaspoon salt

Directions

1. Combine the milk with sugar, tapioca, and salt over moderate heat in a medium-sized saucepan; bring the mix to a boil, stirring constantly. Once done; decrease the heat to low; cook & stir for 5 more minutes.
2. Slowly whisk 1 cup of hot milk mixture into the beaten eggs until incorporated well. Stir the egg mixture into the tapioca mixture again until mixed well.
3. Bring the mix to a gentle simmer; cook & stir until pudding becomes thick enough to evenly coat the back of a metal spoon, for 2 more minutes. Remove from the heat & stir in the vanilla.
4. Serve hot or pour into individual serving dishes & refrigerated for a couple of hours until cold.

Waldorf Pudding

Prep Time: 20 minutes
Cooking Time: 20 minutes
Servings: 16

Ingredients

- 2 cups flour
- ½ cup sugar
- 2 teaspoons baking powder
- 1 cup English walnut meat
- 3 tablespoons melted butter
- 1 cup milk
- 2 eggs
- 1 ½ cups unpeeled apples, diced
- ½ cup steamed raisins
- 1 teaspoon vanilla
- ½ teaspoon salt

For Sauce:
- 2 egg yolks, beaten
- ½ teaspoon lemon extract
- 1 cup sugar
- 2 cups whipped cream
- ½ cup water

Directions

1. Mix the flour with sugar, baking powder and salt; add the eggs with milk, vanilla extract, apples, butter, raisins, and nuts.
2. Mix well & evenly divide into 9 greased individual molds. Using greased papers; cover & steadily steam for 45 minutes. Turn out and serve.

For Sauce:
1. Boil the sugar with water until syrup spins a thread, pour on top of the beaten yolks of eggs; quickly stir and add in the lemon extract.
2. Set aside to cool, stirring occasionally. Just before serving, mix in whipped cream.

Candy

Buckeyes

Prep Time: 20 minutes
Cooking Time: 1 hours & 20 minutes
Servings: 36

Ingredients

- 2 ½ cups confectioners' sugar, sifted
- 1 cup smooth peanut butter
- 8 ounces bittersweet or semisweet chocolate, chopped
- ½ teaspoon pure vanilla extract
- 6 tablespoons unsalted butter, melted
- 1 teaspoon vegetable shortening
- ¼ teaspoon kosher salt

Directions

1. Line a large-sized baking sheet with the parchment. Using an electric mixer in a medium bowl; beat the peanut butter with confectioners' sugar, vanilla, butter, and salt until mixed well. Scoop 2-teaspoonful mounds & roll into small balls; arrange them on the prepared baking sheet & refrigerate for 20 minutes, until firm.
2. Microwave the shortening & chocolate in a microwave-safe medium bowl for 2 minutes, until the mixture is completely smooth & melted, in 30-second increments, stirring in between.
3. Stick a skewer or toothpick into the top center of a peanut butter ball. Dip the ball into the melted chocolate, leaving a circle of peanut butter visible on top. Let any excess chocolate to drip off and then, return the buckeye to the baking sheet. Repeat with the leftover chocolate and peanut butter balls.
4. Let the buckeyes to chill for 30 minutes, until firm. Smooth out the hole left by the toothpick using an offset spatula. Serve at room temperature or well chilled.

Honeycomb Toffee

Prep Time: 20 minutes
Cooking Time: 20 minutes
Servings: 08

Ingredients

- 1 teaspoon baking soda
- 2 tablespoons corn syrup
- ½ cup white sugar
- 1 tablespoon honey
- 2 tablespoons water

Directions

1. Line a large-sized baking dish with the parchment paper, measure out baking soda in a small bowl.
2. Next, whisk the corn syrup with sugar, honey, and water in a saucepan with a candy thermometer attached. Heat until the mixture is thinner but still cloudy, over moderate heat. Let bubble until the thermometer registers 300 degrees F and the mixture is clear.
3. Remove from the heat. Whisk in the baking soda until just incorporated. Switch to a spatula & carefully pour into the lined dish. Let completely cool.
4. Remove the candy from the pan by lifting the parchment paper out. Rap against the counter & break it into individual pieces using your fingers.

Peanut Butter Fudge

Prep Time: 30 minutes
Cooking Time: 20 minutes
Servings: 32

Ingredients

- 1 package brown sugar (16 ounce)
- ½ cup butter
- 1 teaspoon vanilla extract
- ¾ cup peanut butter
- 3 ½ cups confectioners' sugar
- ½ cup milk

Directions

1. Over moderate heat in a medium-sized saucepan; heat the butter until melted and then, stir in the milk and brown sugar. Bring the mix to a boil & cook for 2 minutes, stirring now and then
2. Remove the pot from heat and immediately stir in the vanilla and peanut butter.
3. Fill a large mixing bowl with the confectioners' sugar. Pour in the prepared peanut butter mixture & beat until smooth using an electric mixer.
4. Pour the peanut butter mixture into a large dish. Let chill for an hour, until firm then slice into pieces.

Snickers Salad

Prep Time: 10 minutes
Cooking Time: 10 minutes
Servings: 10

Ingredients

- 1 package instant vanilla pudding (3.4 oz)
- 5 full size Snickers bars, chopped
- 1 cup milk
- ½ cup grapes, cut in half
- 5 apples, chopped
- 1 container Cool Whip (8 oz)
- ½ cup sliced strawberries

Directions

1. Combine the milk with pudding mix in a large-sized mixing bowl until mixed well. Fold in the whipped topping.
2. Once done; immediately add the Snickers, apples, strawberries, and grapes to the bowl; give it a good stir. Refrigerate until needed. Enjoy.

Sign-up Now
and Be Notified of New Books

Website: readbooks.today